Library

Badgers

by Mari Schuh

Bullfrog Books

Ideas for Parents and Teachers

Bullfrog Books let children practice reading informational text at the earliest reading levels. Repetition, familiar words, and photo labels support early readers.

Before Reading

- Discuss the cover photo. What does it tell them?
- Look at the picture glossary together. Read and discuss the words.

Read the Book

- "Walk" through the book and look at the photos. Let the child ask questions. Point out the photo labels.
- Read the book to the child, or have him or her read independently.

After Reading

- Prompt the child to think more. Ask: Have you ever seen a badger? Where were you? What was it doing?

Bullfrog Books are published by Jump!
5357 Penn Avenue South
Minneapolis, MN 55419
www.jumplibrary.com

Library of Congress Cataloging-in-Publication Data

Schuh, Mari C., 1975– author.
  Badgers / by Mari Schuh.
    pages cm. — (My first animal library)
  "Bullfrog Books are published by Jump!"
  Audience: Ages 5–8.
  Audience: K to grade 3.
  Includes index.
  ISBN 978-1-62031-286-5 (hardcover: alk. paper) —
  ISBN 978-1-62496-346-9 (ebook)
  1. Badgers—Juvenile literature. I. Title.
  II. Series: Bullfrog books. My first animal library.
  QL737.C25S337 2016
  599.76'7—dc23

                                    2015025215

Editor: Jenny Fretland VanVoorst
Series Designer: Ellen Huber
Book Designer: Michelle Sonnek
Photo Researcher: Michelle Sonnek

Photo Credits: All photos by Shutterstock except: age fotostock, 18–19; Alamy, cover, 16–17; Corbis, 3, 5, 15; Getty, 22; iStock, 11; SuperStock, 6, 8–9, 10; Thinkstock, 12–13, 24.

Printed in the United States of America at Corporate Graphics in North Mankato, Minnesota.

Table of Contents

A Strong Digger 4

Parts of a Badger 22

Picture Glossary 23

Index 24

To Learn More 24

A Strong Digger

Night is here.

A badger wakes up.
It is time to hunt.

Look! He finds a burrow.
An animal lives there.

claws

The badger digs.
His front feet grab dirt.
His back feet kick
away dirt.

See his short body?
It fits into burrows.

See his long nose?
It sniffs for prey.

What's that?
A ground squirrel!
Time to eat!
Yum!

Oh no! A wolf!

Hiss! Hiss!

The badger shows his teeth.

He gives off a bad smell. Phew!

He can fight.

He is ready.

But the wolf is gone.

Day begins.

Time to go home.

19

The badger is tired.

He rests in his own burrow.

Parts of a Badger

nose
Badgers have a very good sense of smell.

fur
Thick fur and tough skin help keep badgers safe from predators.

claws
A badger uses its long, sharp claws to dig quickly.

tail
Badgers have short, bushy tails.

Picture Glossary

burrow
A tunnel or hole in the ground that animals make or use.

hunt
To look for animals to eat.

ground squirrel
A small, furry animal that lives underground.

prey
Animals that are hunted for food.

Index

burrow 6, 10, 20

day 19

digging 9

eating 12

feet 9

hunting 5

night 4

nose 11

prey 11

smell 15

teeth 15

wolf 14, 16

To Learn More

Learning more is as easy as 1, 2, 3.

1) Go to www.factsurfer.com

2) Enter "badgers" into the search box.

3) Click the "Surf" button to see a list of websites.

With factsurfer.com, finding more information is just a click away.